Accounting Ratio (Multiple Choice Questions and Answers)

Toye Adelaja

Introduction

It has been discovered that multiple choice questions have become integral parts of all financial accounting examinations in the world nowadays. This book includes many multiple choice questions and answers on accounting ratio. The book is designed and prepared for candidates preparing for financial accounting examinations.

It is very useful for students in high schools/secondary schools and tertiary institutions who want to know the rudiments of financial accounting.

The book contains various questions on accounting/financial ratios. Answers and explanations are also provided in the book.

Business professionals and other people who are interested in acquiring accounting knowledge will also find the book beneficial.

1. Blue Sea International Company has a current ratio of 1.3 : 1, and a working capital of $60,000. You are required to calculate its current assets.
A. $60,000 B. $180,000 C. $ 200,000 D. $260,000

2. If a dividend cover of a company is 2.5times, and the dividend per common stock is $0.5. The number of common stock of the company is 500,000. Compute the total earnings available to common stock holders.
A. $600,000 B. $625,000 C. $250,000 D. $500,000

3. Which of the following cannot be used to reduce gearing of a company?
A. Retaining profit
B. Redeeming loan notes
C. Issuing new common stocks
D. Issuing new preferred stocks

4. The following were extracted from the 6th year statement of financial position of AY Ltd. and ZY Ltd.

	AY Ltd. $	ZY Ltd. $
10% loan Notes	10,000	100,000
10% preferred stocks	20,000	50,000
Common stocks	100,000	20,000
Reserves	70,000	30,000
Total Capital	200,000	200,000

Compute gearing ratio for the two companies; AY Ltd and ZY Ltd.
A. 15% and 75%
B. 60% and 56%
C. 75% and 60%
D. 15% and 25%

5. Given that the earnings per share of APM Ltd. is $260 in the 3rd year of operation, and its total earnings for the year is $2,000,000. If its common stock dividend is $13, in how many times can a common dividend be paid from the profit available to common stock holders?
A. 30 times   B. 20 times   C. 762 times   D. 12 times

6. What is the reciprocal of price earnings ratio?
A. Dividend payout ratio
B. Earnings yield
C. Retention ratio
D. Dividend cover

7. If dividend cover of AYY Ltd. is 20, what is her retention ratio?
A. 65%   B. 20%   C. 98%   D. 95%

8. The ratio that indicates the level of protection available to the lenders of long term capital in the form of funds available to pay the interest charges is
A. Dividend cover ratio
B. Earnings per share
C. Interest coverage ratio
D. Retention ratio

9. The capital structure of LLD Plc. requires an adjustment on 31st Dec. 2008. The company made a bonus issue of 3 for 5 shares held. The previous EPS was given as $0.16. Determine the adjusted EPS.
A. $0.1   B. $0.5   C. $20   D. $10

10. The following were extracted from the books of Bigi Plc:

Extracts from Profit & Loss Accounts:

	$'000
Sales	40,000
Profit before tax	10,000
Profit after tax	6,000
Dividend proposed	1,400

Extracts from balance sheet:

	$'000
$1 common stocks capital	7,000
10% convertible debentures	2,000
Total assets	10,000

The market price of the common stock is $5.14 each. You are required to calculate diluted earnings per share if the debentures were converted at one common stock for every $10 debenture.
A. $7.7 B. $0.83 C. $.89 D. $0.85

11. A limited liability company has the following share capital at 31 December 2014.

	$'000
Common stocks of $1 each	5,000
7.5% Preferred stocks of $1	200

The market price of the company's common stock at 31 December 2014 is $1.45. The company's changes in equity accounts for the year ended 31 December 2014 shows:

	$'000	$'000
Profit after tax		470
Preferred dividend	15	
Common dividend	52	67
Retained profit for the year		403

What is the earnings yield (E/Y) as at 31st December 2014?

A. 10.8%

B. 6.3%

C. 6.8%

D. 5.6%

12. The table below shows information extracted from the statement of financial position of two companies, X and Y.

	X	Y
	$'000	$'000
Common stocks	800	900
10% Debentures	600	150
Net Profit	300	650

Which providers of finance would experience the greatest degree of risk in times of falling profits?

A. Debenture holders of company X

B. Debentures holders of company Y

C. Common shareholders of company X

D. Common shareholders of company Y

13. Morgan Plc. Makes a right issue at an issue price of $8 per share. The cum-right price is $10 per share. The theoretical ex-rights price is $9.5 per share. What are the terms of the rights issue?

A. 1 for 3

B. 1 for 2

C. 2 for 1

D. 3 for 1

14. Jedo Plc. has $1 common stock in issue. The company's earnings per share (EPS) for the year just ended is $0.25. The dividend payout ratio for the year is 60% and price earnings (PE) ratio is 20 times. What is the dividend yield ratio of the company?
A. 6% B. 25% C. 30% D. 3%

15. What does the accounts receivable turnover ratio tells us?
A. How many times average A/R is collected
B. How often A/R is collected
C. How long a debt will be remained unpaid
D. How bad debt will be reduced

16. The best ratio to evaluate short-term liquidity is
A. Current ratio
B. Cash ratio
C. Acid test ratio
D. Working capital ratio

17. The ratio that explains how efficiently a companies use their assets to generate revenue is
A. Profit margin
B. Receivable turnover ratio
C. Gearing ratio
D. Asset turnover ratio

18. What ratio can be used to test inefficient buying habit?
A. Mark-up margin
B. Working capital ratio
C. Accounts receivable collection period
D. Inventory turnover ratio

19. The ratio that compares investors' and creditors' stake in a company is called
A. Debt ratio

B. Debt to equity ratio
C. Gearing ratio
D. Capital employed ratio

20. Inventory turnover ratio evaluates
A. A company's ability to buy goods on credit
B. A company's ability to move inventory
C. A company's inventory purchasing efficiency
D. B and C above

21. Acid test ratio formula uses which of the following
A. Inventory
B. Total assets
C. Working capital
D. Cash

22. Which of the following ratio is known as the primary ratio?
A. Earnings per share
B. Current ratio
C. Inventory turnover ratio
D. Return on capital employed ratio

23. A company's statement of financial position reports its current assets and current liabilities as shown below:

Current Assets	$'000
Inventory	274
Trade receivable	243
Prepayments	6
Cash & Bank	16
	539
Current Liabilities	
Trade Payable	196
Accrued Expenses	24
Taxation	59
Dividend declared	30
	309

Which of the following is the working capital ratio and liquidity ratio of the company?
  A. 1.7 : 1 and 0.9 : 1
  B. 0.7 : 1 and 0.1 : 1
  C. 2.5 : 1 and 1 : 1
  D. 3.1 : 1 and 3 : 1

24. In which line of business will you expect the working capital ratio to be higher?
A. Electronics outfit
B. Retail trader
C. Pharmaceutical company
D. Construction Industry

25. What is "Y" in the following equation?
Profit margin × Y/capital Employed = Return on capital employed ratio
  A. Profit after tax
  B. Profit before tax and interest
  C. Sales
  D. Asset turnover

26. The two secondary ratios that make up returns on capital employed ratio are:
A. Current ratio and acid test ratio
B. Asset turnover and inventory turnover ratio
C. Asset turnover and A/R turnover
D. Profit margin and Assets turnover ratio

27. Profit margin × Assets turnover =
A. Earnings yield
B. Earnings ratio
C. Return on capital employed ratio
D. Asset turnover ratio

28. John Smith Plc. has in issue 1,000,000 15% cumulative preferred stocks, which it issued many years ago. In the year ended 31 October 2009, the directors were unable to pay all preferred shares dividend but paid $120,000 and were negotiating with the holders to waive the balance. How much preferred dividend will be considered when calculating earnings per share?
A. $120,000 B. $30,000 C. $150,000 D. $250,000

Use the following information to answer question 29 to 31. The following information was extracted from the balance sheet of Tom Smith plc. as at 31 March 2005:

	$'000
Fixed Assets	318,600
Current Assets:	
Stocks	120,040
Debtors	21,740
Bank & cash Balances	122,240
	582,620
Current Liabilities:	
Trade creditors	166,220
Bank overdraft	3,600
Taxation	15,720
Dividend	30,820
Total current liabilities	216,360
	366,260
Financed by:	
Common stocks at $1 each	118,000
Share premium	56,800
Capital reserves	

	82,460
Revenue reserves	79,000
	336,260

Long-term Liabilities	
10% Debentures	30,000
	366,260

29. Compute debt ratio
A. 48.2%   B. 62.5%   C. 42.3%   D. 50%

30. Compute Debt/Equity ratio
A. 32%   B. 43.3%   C. 64%   D. 73.3%

31. Calculate current ratio
A. 1.6 : 1   B. 1.4 : 1   C. 2.5 : 1   D. 1.2 : 1

32. Which of the following is not a ratio used in measuring short-term solvency and liquidity of companies?
A. Current ratio
B. Accounts receivable collection period
C. Inventory turnover rate
D. Inventory turnover period

33. The amount of earnings per share after adjusting for the effect of all potential common stocks is
A. Earnings yield
B. Price earnings ratio
C. Diluted earnings per share
D. Basic earnings per share

Use the following information to solve questions 34 to 41.
Victory venture has misplaced her final Accounts for the year ended 31 December 2009. The company has decided to reconstruct the accounts from the available data.

At December 31, 2009, stock was valued at $162,000. (This was 20% more than the stock at January 1, 2009).

For the year ended 31 December 2009:
Stock Turnover   10times
Gross profit margin 35%
Net profit margin   22%
Fixed assets turnover 4times
Debtors' days   34 (based on 365days in the year)
Creditors' days 42 (based on 365days in the year)
Current ratio   2.5 : 1

The current assets consist of stock, trade debtors, and bank balance. All sales and purchases were made on credit. The proprietor drew $420,000 from the business during the year.

34. Compute turnover
A. $2,248,615 B. $2,284,615 C.$1,485,000 D. $129,600

35. Calculate cost of sales
A. $1,485,000   B. $485,000 C. $600,502 D. $129,600

36. Calculate Net Profit
A. $502,615 B. $200,000 C. $799,615 D. $326,700

37. What is the value of fixed assets
A. $222,440 B. $571,154 C. $502,615 D. $9,138,460

38. Calculate bank balance
A. $14,660 B. $173,984 C. $434,960 D. $60,146

39. Calculate the total value of current liabilities
A. $173,984 B. $60,146 C. $434,960 D. $162,000

40. Compute the value of Net Assets
A. $832,130 B. $224,001 C. $ 173,984 D. $434,960

41. Calculate trade creditors' balance
A. $1,512,000 B. $135,000 C. $162,000 D. $173,984

42. From the following information, compute the working capital ratio of Adexy Limited.

	$'m
Turnover	2,127.3
Inventory	327.8
Accounts receivable	394.0
Accounts payable	(178.0)
Working capital	543.8

A. 5 : 1   B. 0.3 : 1   C. 4.1 : 1   D. 3.1 : 1

43. Prospects Ltd. which had on January 1, 2006, 5,000,000 common stocks having a market value of $3.5 per share decided on June 1, 2006 to make a right issue of 2 for 5 at a price of $3. The company makes up accounts to December 31 every year. What is the Theoretical ex-rights price?
A. $3.36   B. $2.26   C. $3.5   D. $3

The following information to answer question 44 and 45

PYZ PLC. has 2,000,000 common shares and 50,000 10% preferred shares in issue and its common shares are currently quoted on the stock exchange at a price of $9.6 per share.

PYZ PLC made a post-tax profit of $2,450,000.

44. What is earnings per share?
A. $1.22   B. $2.25   C. $0.49   D. 0.44

45. What is price earnings ratio?

A. $8.367   B. $7.87 C. $0.13 D. $2.18

46. Given that in Quarter 2, opening inventory is $110,000 and closing inventory is $80,000. The inventory turnover ratio for the same period is 2. What is the value of purchases in Quarter 2?
A. $120,000 B. $190,000 C. $80,000 D. $160,000

47. What ratio is represented by the formula below?

Shareholders' funds/Total assets × 100
A. Gearing ratio B. Debt/Equity ratio C. Leverage ratio
D. Proprietary ratio

48. 3Y Limited has one million common shares of $1 each in issue. Its profit and loss accounts for the year ended 31st December 2004 showed:

	$
Profit before tax	600,000
Taxation at 30%	(180,000)
Profit after tax	420,000
Earnings per share	$0.42
Price Earnings ratio	8.00

What is the total market value of the company?
A. $3,360,000 B. $260,000 C. $620,000 D. $19,047,619

49. What is the reciprocal of dividend cover?
A. Earnings per share
B. Earnings yield
C. Dividend payout ratio
D. Dividend yield

50. What is the reciprocal of earnings yield?
A. Earnings per share
B. Price earnings ratio
C. Retention ratio
D. Dividend yield

51. One of the benefits of using accounting ratio is that they
A. are easy to calculate
B. facilitate decision-making
C. are stipulated by law
D. show errors and frauds.

52. Given

Cost of sales	$250,000
Sales	$320,000

The gross profit mark- up is
    A. 23% B. 28% C. 22% D. 15%

Use the following information to answer question 3 to 6.

	$	$
Sales		250,000
Opening stocks	?	
Purchases	100,000	
Less: Closing stocks	80,000	
Cost of sales	?	
Gross profit		?

The gross profit margin for the above information is 25%.

53. Calculate cost of sales.
A. $250,000 B. $187,500 C. $190,000 D. $120,000

54. Compute gross profit
A. $80,000 B. $62,500 C. $46,875 D. $18,000

55. Compute Gross profit mark-up
A. 25% B. 30% C. 22.22% D. 33.33%

56. Calculate the opening stock.
A. $167,500 B.$ 67,500 C. $187,500 D. $100,000

57. Calculate stock turnover rate
A. 1.5times B. 2.5times C. 3times D. 6times

Use the following to answer questions 5 to 7

	$
Net profit	80,000
Total Assets	600,000
Current Liabilities	180,000
Current Assets	310,000

58. The current ratio is
A. 1.72 : 1 B. 0.6 : 1 C. 1:2 D. 7.2 : 1

59. The capital employed is
A. $150,000 B. $420,000 C. $310,000 D. $130,000

60. The return on capital employed is
A. 61.54% B. 25.8% C.19.05% D. 1.72%

61. A low current asset ratio in a business indicates that the business is
A. Able to use its resources efficiently
B. Unable to pay its short-term bills as at when due
C. Able to meets its short-term loan
D. Keeping its assets

62. Which of the following best measure the ability of a firm to meet its short-term financial obligation?
A. Current ratio B. stock turn over C. acid test ratio D. creditor payment period

Use the following information to answer question 13 – 17
The balance sheet extract of Jane Limited is given as follows:

	2009	2008
	$'000	$'000
Cash	1,130	-
Investment (marketable security)	860	750
Accounts receivable	5,030	5,350
Inventory	7,900	6,500
	14,920	12,600
Trade Creditors	-7,730	-7,150
Bank overdraft		-360
	7,190	5,090

63. Compute current ratio for the year 2009 and 2008 respectively.

    A. 1.93 and 1.68 B.1 and 1.2 C.0.9 and 1.9 D.1.68 and 1.93

64. Compute quick ratio for the year 2009 and 2008 respectively.
    A.0.98 and 1 B. 1.5 and 2 C.1 and 2 D. 0.91 and 0.81

65. Compute acid test ratio for year 2009.
    A.0.91: 1 B. 0.81:1 C. 1 : 0.8 D. 2 : 1

66. Calculate working capital for year 2009 and 2008 respectively.
    A. $660 and $750 B.$ 7,730 and $7,510 C. $7,190 and $5,090
    D. $5,090 and $7,190

67. Compute cash ratio for year 2009.
    A. 0.4: 1 B.1.2:1 C. 2: 1 D. 0.26: 1

68. The price-earnings ratio for a company with earnings per share of $4.32 is 11. If the total number of shares in issue is 60,000, what is the total market value of the share?
    A. $2,851,200 B. $2,852,100 C. $23,564 D. $259,200

69. The ratio expressing the relationship between debt capital and Equity holders' funds is called
    A. debt ratio   B. interest cover   C. proprietor ratio   D. gearing ratio

70. Which of the following will be excluded from the calculation of acid test ratio?
    A. cash at hand   B. bank balance   C. inventory   D. accounts receivable

Use the following information to answer question 20 to 24. J.J. Ltd., during the current accounting period, had sales (all on credit) of $415,000 and cost of goods sold of $262,500. At the beginning of the year, its Accounts Receivable were $40,000 and its inventory was $50,000. At the end of the year, its Accounts Receivable were $43,000 and its inventory was $55,000.

71. Compute accounts receivable collection period
    A. 42 days   B. 37 days   C. 27 days   D.40 days

72. Compute accounts receivable turnover
    A. 9 times   B.11 times   C. 13 days   D. 10 times

73. Stock turnover rate is
    A. 5 times   B. 7 times   C. 73 times   D. 1825days

74. Stock turnover period is
    A. 37days   B. 73 days   C. 83 days   D.73 times

75. Victory company Ltd. has a debt-to-equity ratio of 1.9 compared with the industry average of 1.5. This means that the company
    A. has less liquidity than other firm
    B. has higher credit worthiness than the industrial average
    C. Will be able to meet its financial obligation earlier than other firms in the industry
    D. has greater financial risk than other firms in the industry

Use the following information to answer questions 26 to 31. The following were extracted from the books of Jendo International Ltd.

	2014	2013
	$	$
Net profit after taxation	24,960	21,940
Dividend proposed	-12,000	-11,500
Retained profit	12,960	10,440

An extract from the statement of financial position (balance sheet) as at 31st December, 2014

	2014	2013
	$	$
Common stock of $1 each	50,000	42,000
Share premium	18,000	18,000
Capital reserves	22,000	22,000
Revenue reserves	32,000	25,000
	122,000	107,000
Non-current liabilities		
10% debenture	15,000	15,000
	137,000	122,000

NOTE: The market price of the company's share has been fairly stable at $4 per share. Taxation for year 2014 and 2013 were $10,697 and $9,403 respectively.

76. Calculate earning per share for the year 2014 and 2013 respectively from the above information
A. $0.22 and $1.67   B. $0.499 and $0.522   C. $1.2 and $2.1

77. Compute dividend per share for year 2014 and 2013 respectively
A. $0.24 and $0.274   B. $0.50 and $0.52   C. $0.274 and $0.24
D.$2 and $1.5

78. Compute dividend cover for year 2014 and year 2013 respectively
A. 3.5times and 2.5times B. 0.48times and 0.53times
C. 2.08 times and 1.91times   D. 3times and 2times

79. Compute dividend yield for year 2014 and year 2013 respectively
A. 6% and 6.85% B. 20% and 30%
C. 14% and 12%   D. 0.3times and 2.3times

80. Calculate earnings yield for year 2013
A. 21.1% B. 13.05% C. 22% D. 18%

81. Calculate return on capital employed for year 2013
A. 22% B. 23% C. 20.51% D. 26.92%

82. Compute gearing ratio for the year 2014
A. 2% B.112% C. 12% D. 14%

83. Which of the following is an effect of highly geared company?
A. It encourages employees
B. It discourages employees
C. It discourages creditors and investors
D. It boosts the income

84. The market price of PTV Company's ordinary shares increase from $4 to $6. Earning per share remained constant. The company's price-earnings ratio would
A. decrease B. be constant C. increase D. non of the above

85. Somopex & company ltd. has a current ratio of 1.2 : 1 The current ratio later decreased to 1:1. Which of the following is a cause of the decrease?
A. payment of accounts payable
B. collection of accounts receivable
C. additional bad debt written off
D. Purchase of inventory for cash

86. The only assets possessed by a company are inventory $2,500,000, cash at bank $250,000, and receivables $1,200,000. The current ratio of the company is 2:1. What is the quick ratio?
A. 0.67: 1   B. 0.73:1   C. 0.33:1   D. 2:1

87. Which of the following is a formula for calculating interest cover?
A. profit before interest and tax divided by interest
B. profit minus interest plus tax divided by interest
C. Interest divided by profit plus interest and tax
D. Interest divided by Net profit

88. Which of the following ratio is not used in measuring short term solvency and liquidity of a company?
A. cash ratio   B. current ratio   C. quick ratio   D. Net cash flow ratio

89. Which of the following is not a ratio for measuring long-term solvency of a company?
A. debt ratio   B. gearing ratio   C. interest cover   D. dividend cover

90. Earnings yield is an example of which ratio?
A. Shareholders Investment ratio   B. solvency ratio   C. liquidity ratio   D. activity ratio

Answers

1	D	21	D	41	D	61	B	81	D
2	B	22	D	42	C	62	C	82	C
3	D	23	A	43	A	63	A	83	C
4	A	24	D	44	A	64	D	84	C
5	B	25	C	45	B	65	A	85	C
6	B	26	D	46	D	66	C	86	B
7	D	27	C	47	D	67	D	87	A
8	C	28	C	48	A	68	A	88	D
9	A	29	C	49	C	69	D	89	D
10	B	30	D	50	C	70	C	90	A
11	B	31	D	51	B	71	B		
12	C	32	C	52	B	72	D		
13	A	33	C	53	B	73	A		
14	D	34	B	54	B	74	B		
15	B	35	A	55	D	75	D		
16	B	36	A	56	A	76	B		
17	D	37	B	57	A	77	A		
18	D	38	D	58	A	78	C		
19	B	39	A	59	B	79	A		
20	D	40	A	60	C	80	B		

WORKINGS:

Working 1

Calculation of Current Assets

Current ratio = 1.3 : 1

Working capital = $60,000

Cr = CA/CL

CA = Cr × CL

CA = 1.3 × CL   equation i

CA - CL = $60,000

CA = $60,000 + CL equation ii

CA = CA

1.3 × CL = $60,000 + CL

1.3CL - CL = $60,000

0.3CL = $60,000

CL = $60,000/0.3

CL = $200,000

Substitute $200,000 for CL in equation i

CA = 1.3 × CL
CA = 1.3 × $200,000

CA = $260,000

Current Assets = $260,000

Where :
CA = Current Assets
CL = Current Liabilities
Cr = Current ratio

Working 2

Computation of earnings available to common stock holders:

Dividend cover = EPS/DPS

DC = EPS/DPS

EPS = DC × DPS

   = 2.5 × $0.5

   = $1.25

Total earnings available to common stockholders
= Common stocks × EPS
= 500,000 × $1.25
= $625,000

<u>Working 4</u>
Computation of gearing ratios for the two companies:
Where:
Gr = Gearing ratio
PCC = Prior charge capital
TC = Total capital

Gr = PCC/TC × 100

Gearing ratio for AY Ltd.:

Gr = PCC/TC × 100

Gr = $30,000/$200,000 × 100

   = 15%

Gearing ratio for ZY Ltd. :

$Gr = PCC/TC \times 100$

$Gr = \$150,000/\$200,000 \times 100$

$= 75\%$

Working 5

Dividend Cover
= EPS/DPS
= \$260/\$13
= 20 times

Working 7
Computation of retention ratio:
Retention ratio:
$Rr = 1 - $ payout ratio

$Rr = 1 - 1/DC$

$Rr = 1 - 1/20$

$Rr = 0.95$

$Rr = 95\%$

Where:
Rr = Retention ratio
DC = Divided Cover

Working 9

Adjusted EPS

= Existing shares × Previous EPS

Total no. of shares
   $= 5/3+5 \times \$0.16$
   $= \$0.1$

Working 10

Diluted Earnings Per Share:

$=$ PAT + Interest saved/Total shares

Where :
Total shares = Existing shares + New shares
PAT = Profit available to common stock holders

Diluted Earnings per share :

$=$ PAT + Interest saved/Total shares

$= 6,000,000/7,000,000 + 200,000$

$= \$0.83$

Working 11

Earnings yield = EPS/MPS $\times$ 100

Calculation of EPS:

EPS = PAT – Preferred dividend/Number of common stocks

$= \$470,000 - \$15,000/5,000,000$

$= \$455,000/5,000,000$

= $0.091

Earnings yield:

= EPS/MPS × 100

= $0.091/$1.45 × 100

= 6.3%

<u>Working 14</u>

Dividend yield:

DY = DPS/MPS × 100
The value of dividend per share (DPS) and Market price per share (MPS) are not given in the information provided in the question, and hence they should be calculated.

Payout ratio = 1/Dividend cover

$$
\begin{aligned}
60\% \quad &= 1/DC \\
0.6 \quad &= 1/DC \\
0.6DC &= 1 \\
DC \quad &= 1/0.6
\end{aligned}
$$

The formula for the calculation of dividend cover is stated below:

DC   = EPS/DPS

1/0.6   = $0.25/DPS

DPS   = 0.6 × $0.25

* DPS   = $0.15

The formula for calculating price earnings ratio is stated below:

PER= MPS/EPS

MPS/$0.25 = 20/1

MPS　　　= 20 × $0.25

* MPS　　= $5

Calculation of Dividend yield

DY　= DPS/MPS × 100

　　= $0.15/$5 × 100

　　= 0.03 × 100
　3%

The Dividend Yield is 3%

Where:
DPS = Dividend per share
MPS = Market price per share
EPS = Earnings per share
DC = Dividend cover
PER = Price earnings ratio

Working 23

Computation of Working Capital Ratio

WCR = CA/CL

    = \$539,000/\$309,000

    = 1.74

    = 1.7 : 1

Where:

WCR = Working capital ratio

CA = Current Assets

CL = Current Liabilities

Computation of Liquidity Ratio

LR= (CA − Inventory)/CL

    = \$(539,000 − 274,000)/\$309,000

    = 0.857

    = 0.9 : 1

Working 29

Debt ratio = Total debt/Total Assets

        = (216,360 + 30,000)/582,620

        = 42.3%

Working 30

Debt Equity ratio

= Total debt/Equity

= (216,360 +30,000)/336,260

= 73.3%

Working 31

Current ratio = CA/CL

$$= \$264,020/\$216,360$$

$$= 1.2$$

$$= 1.2 : 1$$

Working 34

Calculation of turnover or Sales:
Closing stock = Opening stock ×120%
$162,000　　= Opening stock × 1.2
$162,000/1.2 = Opening stock × 1.2/1.2

$135,000　　= Opening stock

Opening stock is $135,000

Stock turnover = COS/AVS

10　　= COS/$(135,000 + 162,000)/2

10　　= COS/$148,500

COS　= $148,500 × 10

COS　= $1,485,000

* Cost of sales = $1,485,000

Where:
COS = Cost of sales
AVS = Average stock

Gross profit margin = 35%
Gross profit margin can be converted to gross profit mark-up as follows:
Gross profit margin = P/S

Gross profit mark-up = P/ S-P

Gross profit mark-up = P/COS

$$= 35/100\text{-}35$$

$$= 35/65$$

35/65	= P/$1,485,000
65P	= 35 × $1,485,000
P	= $51,975,000/65
* P	= $799,615

Gross profit is $799,615.

Where:
P = Gross profit
COS = Cost of sales
S = Sales

We can now compute the value of turnover (sales) having calculated the cost of sales and gross profit.

Turnover = Cost of sales + Gross profit

Turnover = $1,485,000 + $799,615

Turnover = $2,284,615

Working 35

The cost of sales is $1,485,000. This can be seen in the part of working 34.

Working 36

Calculation of Net profit:

Net profit margin = 22%

22/100	= NP/Sales
	= NP/$2,284,615

100NP	= 22 × $2,284,615

NP	= $50,261,530/100

NP	= $502,615

Where:
NP = Net profit

Working 37

Calculation of the value of Fixed Assets:

Fixed assets turnover = 4times

Fixed assets turnover = sales/FA

Sales/FA = 4times

$2,284,615/FA = 4

4 FA	= $2,284,615
FA	= $2,284,615/4
FA	= $571,154

Where:
FA = Fixed Assets
Fixed assets can also be referred to as non- current assets.

Working 38

Calculation of bank balance:

According to the information given, current assets consist of stock, debtors, and bank balance.

Bank balance :
= CA – (Stock balance + Debtors' balance)

We need to calculate debtors' balance and total current assets. Stock balance has already been calculated to be $162,000.

Debtors' balance
Debtors/sales × 365days = 34days

Debtors/$2,284,615 × 365days = 34days

365days × Debtors = $2,284,615 × 34days

Debtors   = $77,676,910days/365days

Debtors   = $212,813.45

*Debtors   = $212,814

Trade creditors' balance which is the total current liability according to the information available should be calculated.

Trade creditor's balance

Creditors/credit purchases × 365days = 42days

Credit purchases must be calculated because it is not given in the question.

Calculation of credit purchases:

	$
Opening stocks	135,000
Purchases	?
Cost of goods available	135,000 + ?
Less closing stocks	162,000
Cost of sales	1,485,000

(135,000 + ?) - $162,000 = $1,485,000

? - $27,000 = $1,485,000
?   =$1,485,000 + $27,000

?   = $1,512,000

Purchases = $1,512,000

Credit purchases is $1,512,000

Calculation of trade creditors' balance:

Creditors/Credit purchases × 365days = 42days

Creditors/$1,512,000 × 365days = 42days

365days × creditors = $1,512,000 × 42days

365 × creditors = $63,504,000

Creditors   = $63,504,000/365

Creditors   = $173,983.56

According to the information available in the question, trade creditors are equal to total current liabilities. It is now easy to calculate total current assets because total current liabilities have been computed, and current ratio is already given in the question.

Current ratio = CA/CL

Current ratio = 2.5

CA/CL = 2.5

CA/$173,984 = 2.5

CA   = 2.5 × $173,984

CA   = $434,960

Where:
CA = Current Assets

CL = Current Liabilities

Finally, we can now calculate bank balance.

Stock balance + Debtors + y = current assets

$162,000 + $212,814 + y= $434,960

$374,814 + y   =$434,960

y   =$434,960 - $374,814

y   = $60,146

Bank balance is $60,146

Where:
y = Bank balance

Working 40

Computation of Net Assets:
Net Assets = TA – TL
TA = FA + CA
   = $571,154 +$434960
   = $1,006,114
TL = $173,984

Net Assets = $1,006,114 - $173,984
        = $832,130

Working 42

Computation of working capital ratio

WCR   = CA/CL

      = \$(327.8m +394m)/\$178m

      = \$721.8m/\$178m

      = 4.06

      = 4.1 : 1

Where:
CA = Current Assets

CL = Current Liabilities

Working 43

Computation of theoretical ex-right price

TERP =(VES + VNS)/TNS

      = \$(3.5 × 5,000,000 + 3 ×2,000,000)/7,000,000

      =\$(17,500,000 + 6,000,000)/7,000,000

      = \$23,500,000/7,000,000

      = \$3.357

      = \$3.36

Where:
TERP = Theoretical ex-right price
VES = Value of existing shares
VNS = value of new shares
TNS = Total number of shares

Working 44

Calculation of earnings per share

EPS = (PAT- preferred dividend)/TNS

$$= \$(2{,}450{,}000 - 5{,}000)/2{,}000{,}000$$

$$= \$2{,}445{,}000/2{,}000{,}000$$

$$= \$1.2225$$

$$= \$1.22$$

Where:
EPS = Earnings per share
PAT = Profit after tax
TNS = Total Number of common shares

Working 45

Calculation of price earning ratio

PER = MPS/EPS

$$= \$9.6/\$1.22$$

$$= \$7.87$$

Where:
PER = price earnings ratio
MPS = Market price per share
EPS = Earnings per share

Working 46

Calculation of value of purchases in Quarter 2:
Inventory turnover ratio
ITR = COS/AVS

It is given in the information available that the inventory
turnover ratio is 2.
ITR = 2

COS/AVS = 2

COS/(110,000 + 80,000)/2 = 2/1

COS/95,000   = 2/1

COS   = $190,000

Calculation of purchases

	$
Opening Inventory	110,000
Purchases	y
	110,000 + y
Less closing	(80,000)
Cost of sales	190,000

$110,000 + y -$80,000 = $190,000

$30,000 + y   = $190,000

Y   = $190,000 - $30,000

Y   = $160,000

Purchase for the Quarter 2 is $160,000

Where:
COS = Cost of sales
AVS = Average stock
ITR = Inventory turnover ratio
y   = Purchases

Working 48

Calculation of the total market value of the company:

Market price per share should first be calculated.

$PER = MPS/EPS$

$PER = 8$

$PER = MPS/EPS$
$MPS/EPS = 8$
$MPS/\$0.42 = 8/1$

$MPS = 8 \times \$0.42$

$MPS = \$3.36$

Total market value of the company is calculated below:

= Number of common shares × MPS

= 1,000,000 × $3.36

= $3,360,000

52.

$320,000 – $250,000 = $70,000

Gross Profit mark-up:
= Gross profit/ Cost of sales
= $70,000/$250,000 × 100%
= 28%

53.
Gross profit = 25/100×250,000 = $62,500

Cost of sales = Sales – Gross profit
                     = $250,000 – $62,500
                     = $187,500

55.
Gross profit mark-up:

= $62,500/$187,500 × 100
= 33.33%

57. Stock turnover rate
= cost of sales/Average stock
= $187,500/$123,750
= 1.5 times

58. Current ratio = current asset/ current liability

          = $310,000/$180,000

          = 1.72:1

59. Capital employed = Total assets – Current liabilities
                     = $600,000 – $180,000
                     = $420,000

60. Return on capital employed:

$= $ Net profit/ Capital employed $\times$ 100%

$= \$80,000/\$420,000 \times 100\%$

$= 19.05\%$

64. Quick ratio $=$ (Current assets - inventory)/ Current liability

2009

Quick ratio $= \$(14,920 - 7,900)/ \$ 7,190$

$= 0.98$

2008

Quick ratio $= \$(12,600-6,500)/\$7,510$

$= 0.81$

65. Acid test ratio is the same as quick ratio (0.98: 1)

66. Working capital $=$ Current Assets – Current Liabilities

67. Cash ratio $=$ (cash + cash equivalent)/ current Asset

$= \$(1,130 + 860)/ \$7,730$

$= 0.26:1$

68. Price-earnings ratio $=$ MPS/ EPS

MPS/$ 4.32 = $11

MPS = $47.52

Total market value of the share:

= $47.52×60,000
= $2,851,200

NOTE:
MPS = Market price per share,
EPS = Earning per share

71. ARCP = AVAR/ SALES × 365days

$$= \frac{\$(40,000 + 43,000)/2}{\$415,000} \times 365days$$

= 37days

NOTE: ARCP = Accounts Receivable Collection Period
AVR = Average Accounts Receivable

72. Accounts receivable turnover

= Sales/ AVAR

= $415,000/$41,500

= 10times

73. Stock turnover rate = COS/ AVS

= $262,500/$(50,000 + 55,000)/2

= 5 times

NOTE:

COS = Cost of sales,

AVS =Average stock

74. Stock turnover period = AVS/ COS × 365 days

$$= \frac{\$(50{,}000 + 55{,}000)/2}{\$262{,}500}$$

= 73 days

76.   2014   2013

EPS = NPATP/NCS

EPS =$24,960/50,000   = $21,940/42,000

=$0.499   = $0.522

Note:
EPS = earnings per shares
NPATP = Net profit after tax and preference dividend (preferred stock)
NCS   = Numbers of ordinary shares (common stocks)

Net profit after tax and preference dividend is the profit available to common stockholders.

77.   2014   2013

Dividend per share = Dividend/ Number of ordinary shares

= $12,000/50,000   = $11,500/42,000

= $0.24   = $0.274

78.   2014   2013

Dividend cover = Earnings per share/ Dividend per share

= $0.499/$0.24   = $0.522/$0.274

=2.08times   =1.91times

79.   2014   2013

Dividend yield:

= Dividend per share/ Market price per share ×100%

= $0.24/$4 × 100%   = $0.274/ $4 × 100%

= 6%   = 6.85%

80. Earnings yield for year 2013:

= Earnings per share/ Market price per share × 100%

= $0.522/$4 × 100%

= 13.05%

81. Return on capital employed for the year 2013:

Profit before interest and tax/ Capital employed × 100%

= ($21,940 +$1,500 + $9,403)/$122,000 × 100%

= 26.92%

82. Gearing ratio for year 2014:

$\quad$ = Prior charge capital/ Total equity ×100

$\quad$ = $15,000/$122,000 ×100

$\quad$ = 0.12295 ×100

$\quad$ = 0.12 ×100

$\quad$ = 12%

86. Current assets:
$\quad$ = $2,500,000 +$250,000+$1,200,000
$\quad$ = $3,950,000

Current ratio = Current assets/Current liabilities

$\quad$ Current ratio = 2

$\quad$ Current assets/ Current liabilities = 2/1

$\quad$ $ 3,950,000/ Current Liabilities   = 2/1

$\quad$ Current liabilities = $1,975,000

Quick Ratio = ($3,950,000 – $2,500,000)/$1,975,000

$\quad\quad$ = 0.73

$\quad\quad$ = 0.73 : 1

www.ingramcontent.com/pod-product-compliance
Lightning Source LLC
Chambersburg PA
CBHW061228180526
45170CB00003B/1214